Shellcraft

W9-CPK-375

To Laurine, Yohann and Élise

Shellcraft

Annette and Roger Ralle

SEARCH PRESS

First published in Great Britain 1999 by
Search Press Limited
Wellwood
North Farm Road
Tunbridge Wells
Kent TN2 3DR

Originally published in France 1997 by
Éditions Didier CARPENTIER
Original title: *Un Petit Monde en Coquillages*
Copyright © Éditions Didier CARPENTIER 1997

English translation by Norman Porter
English translation © Search Press Limited 1999

The publishers would like to thank Noel Gregory for his help
in the translation of shell names.

All rights reserved. No part of this book, text, photographs
or illustrations may be reproduced or transmitted in any
form or by any means by print, photoprint, microfilm,
microfiche, photocopier or in any way known or as yet
unknown, or stored in a retrieval system, without written
permission obtained beforehand from Search Press.

ISBN 0 85532 894 0

Readers are permitted to reproduce any of the items/
patterns in this book for their personal use, or for the
purposes of selling for charity, free of charge and without
the prior permission of the Publishers. Any use of the items/
patterns for commercial purposes is not permitted without
the prior permission of the Publishers.

The designs shown in this book have been created and
constructed by the authors. Some of the more simple ones
have been successfully and enthusiastically tested by
children from Ile de Noirmoutier, namely pupils of the class
of Jean-Paul Gauthier. He is headmaster of the State School
of La Gueriniere.

Printed in Hong Kong through Printworks Int. Ltd.

Contents

Rissoa
Rissoa Parva

Dwarf winkle
Littorina
Neritoides

Pheasant
Tricolia
Pullus

Cerith
Cerithium
Rupestre

Cylinder
Cylichna
Cylindraea

Mangelia
Mangelia
Nebula

Green sea urchin
Echinocyamus
Pusillus

Small dog whelk
Nassarius
Pygmaea

Nut
Nucula
Nucleus

European cowrie
Trivia Artica

Netted dog whelk
Nassarius Reticulata

Acteon
Acteon Tornatelis

Wentletrap
Epitonium Clathrus

Thin tellin
Argulus Tenuis

Edible winkle
Littorina Littorea

Baltic tellin
Macoma Baltica

Lurid cowrie
Luria Lurida

Spotted cowrie
Erosaria Spurca

Painted top
Caliostoma Zizyphinum

Sting winkle
Ocenebra Erinacea

Necklace
Natica Catena

Pelican's foot
Aporrhais Pespelecani

Thick trough
Spisula Solida

Limpet
Patella Vulgata

Cockle
Cerastoderma Edule

Mussel
Mytilus Edulis

Banded carpet
Paphia Rhomboides

Dosinia
Dosinia Exoleta

Queen scallop
Pecten Opercularis

Rayed trough
Mactra Stultorium

Oyster
Crassostrea Gigas

Gaper
Mya Arenaria

Common otter
Lutraria Lutraria

Lutraria
Lutraria Angustior

European cowrie
Trivia Monacha

Rough winkle
*Littoria
Saxatilis*

Grey top
*Gibbula
Cineraria*

White abra
Abra Alba

Chinese hat
*Calptraea
Chinensis*

Purple top
*Gibbula
Mmbilicalis*

Flat winkle
*Littorina
Obtusata*

Nassa
Nassarius Cuvieri

Large top
Gibbula Magus

Tiger scallop
Pallioluim Tigerinum

Bulla
Bulla Striata

Tusk
Dentalium Entalis

Dog whelk
Nucella Lapillus

Tower
Turritela Communis

Banded wedge
Donax Vittatus

Rayed cockle
Cardium Paucicostata

Tellin
Tellina Tenuis

Saddle oyster
Anomia Ephippium

Goose barnacle
Lepas Anatifera

Angel wings
Pholas Dactylus

Worm
Vermetes Semisurrectus

Variegated scallop
Chlamys Varia

Rock barnacle
Balanus Crenatus

Sea urchin
Psammechinus Milaris

Pullet carpet
Venerupis Senegalensis

Slipper limpet
Crepidula Fornicata

Whelk
Buccinum Undatum

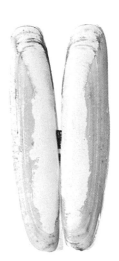

Grooved razor
Solen Marginatus

Egg shell razor
Pharus Legumen

Sword razor
Ensis Ensis

Large cockle
Cardium Tuberculata

General advice

Materials

Apart from shells illustrated on pages 6 and 7, which you can collect whole or in pieces, there are a few other marine items will come in useful.

Fish bones

These will not normally be found on a beach but you could use bones that you would normally throw away after eating fish. Gather together the bones, wash them in water with a drop of washing-up liquid and leave them to dry. The most interesting bones are situated towards the fish's head. Tuna bones are quite straight but they are fragile. The bones of bream and red or grey mullet are curved and thick. Salmon bones are slightly curved, fine and delicate.

Sea urchins

The carapaces (tests) of sea urchins can be found on beaches. If you look carefully you can find whole tests but they are very fragile so handle them carefully.

Starfish

The starfish is an animal and not a shellfish. If you want to avoid unpleasant smells, you must leave it to soak for a few days in a closed jar containing formalin – a substance which dehydrates organic matter. Formalin (as used in agriculture) can be obtained from hardware stores. Follow the manufacturer's instructions carefully when using it and take precautions such as wearing gloves, an apron and protective glasses. Rinse the treated starfish thoroughly and then let it dry. The residual smell of formalin disappears after a few days.

> ### COLLECTING SHELLS
>
> *1. Whenever you go to the seaside take a bag or container in which to collect shells and other interesting marine items.*
>
> *2. Only collect shells which are empty, clean and odour-free.*
>
> *3. Some shells are very fragile. Wrap them in tissue paper to avoid damage.*
>
> *4. Do not ignore shells or pieces of shell which look uninspiring. You may well find a use for them later on.*
>
> *5. Do not only collect the large shells. Small shells, and even very tiny ones can all be put to good use when making models. Keep these in a separate container.*
>
> *6. Search for a variety of shells. Your collection for model making should include a wide range of types, shapes, sizes and colours.*
>
> *7. Wash the shells in clean water as soon as possible and leave them to dry.*
>
> *8. Sort the shells into different groups and store them in boxes or trays. When you start to make a model, you will then be able to select the right shells quickly and easily.*
>
> *9. A glossary of special words to describe parts of shells is included on page 63.*

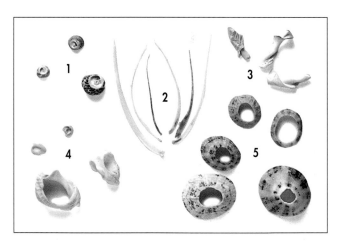

1. Truncations of top shells   2. Fish bones
3. Columella   4. Peristomes   5. Limpet rings

Equipment

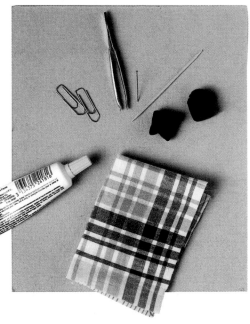

nor too fragile, have been suggested. Most of the designs balance well on three, spread-out points of contact. Others are secured to a firm base.

Some of the more sophisticated models require greater dexterity. Be prepared to work in several stages, waiting for each element to set properly before continuing with the composition.

The models in this book have been constructed without any skeleton, metallic framework or integral support. Sometimes, you will need to use templates to create particular shapes, but these temporary supports are removed after drying.

- Sheet of cardboard or wood to protect the table
- General purpose glue, with a reasonably fast drying time
- Rag
- Cocktail stick to apply drops of glue
- Pin to clean the inside of certain shells
- Tweezers
- Modelling clay or similar material for supporting models during assembly.

Assembly

Much of the gluing and assembly can be done on a flat work surface. Lots of the models included in this book can be completed in one session. However, for others it will be necessary to assemble part of a model and then leave the glue to set really hard before finally completing it. Remember that while the glue is setting (and it may need to be left overnight to be effective) the weight of some shells might upset the rest of the structure. The models included in this book have been designed to help avoid this problem. Only easy-to-handle shells, which are neither too heavy

GLUING SHELLS

1. Protect the work surface with a sheet of carboard or wood.

2. Always have a rag available for wiping your hands and for removing unwanted glue.

3. Handle tubes of glue carefully so the glue does not run too quickly. Always replace the lid after each application of glue.

4. Always wait until a composition is properly set before proceeding with the assembly.

5. Check regularly that the composition is not sticking to the work surface or template, nor to any supports.

6. If you want to varnish your model, wait twenty-four hours until the glue is really dry, then apply a coat of clear gloss varnish with a small paint brush.

7. Finally, always be patient!

Small objects with cockles

If you ask a child to draw a shell, they will almost certainly sketch the shape of a cockle. This simple yet characterful shell can be readily adapted to make small, charming objects.

The saltcellar, an age-old article, made from shells.

Saltcellar

Materials

- Flat oyster valve for the base
- Whole cockle
- Sting winkle

Method

Place the two halves of the cockle side by side, flat on the work surface, then glue them together. When the assembly is rigid enough to be handled, turn it over and fix it to the oyster shell. If necessary, provide support during the drying process. Finally, glue the sting winkle between the two halves of the cockle to act as a handle.

Desk tidy

Materials

- Three large cockle valves
- Four acteons to make the trunk of the palm tree handle
- Six banded wedge valves and a limpet for the leaves

You can decorate your desk tidy with any small shells you have available.

Method

Glue the three large cockle valves together in a similar way to those for the saltcellar. Build up the trunk of the palm tree by gluing the acteons end to end. Place the banded wedge valves, hollow side downwards, on the work surface, arrange them in a star shape and glue them together. Cover the centre join with a limpet. When the leaves are dry, glue them on top of the trunk.

Awèlé

Materials

- Six whole large cockles for the holders
- Forty-eight very small shells (cowries or top shells) for use as seeds (counters)

Method

Place the large cockle valves flat on the work surface and arrange them in two rows of six. Glue them together and then leave them to dry for twenty-four hours. Turn the whole assembly over and strengthen it with an additional application of glue between the shells. When dry the twelve holders will be solid so it is not necessary to fix them to a base.

Awèlé is an African thinking game. It is played with two players but these players will soon find themselves surrounded by spectators commenting on their moves and giving them advice.

RULES OF THE GAME OF AWÈLÉ

Awèlé is a game for two players. Each player has a row of six cups, with four seeds in each cup. The object of the game is to capture most seeds.

A player takes all the seeds from one of his cups and, working in an anti-clockwise direction, places them, one by one, in consecutive cups. When the number of seeds collected allows the player to go round the board more than once, he must miss out the cup from which the seeds were taken. If the cup in which the last seed is placed belongs to the opponent and now contains two or three seeds, the player captures those seeds. He also captures the seeds in the previous cup if that only contains two or three seeds, and so on, until he comes to one that has fewer than two or more than three, or until he comes to the end of the opponent's row. The captured seeds are set aside. Then it is the turn of the other player to sow.

The game ends when a player has no seeds to sow. For scoring purposes, the seeds left in the cups are added to the captured seeds. The winner is the player who has the most seeds. As far as possible the player should 'feed' his opponent's cups, to avoid them becoming empty.

On the pond

Swan

Materials

- Dog whelk for the body
- Small dog whelk for the head
- Five pieces of goose barnacle for the wings, tail and neck

Method

Use a pair of tweezers to break off the end of a long thin piece of goose barnacle to create the swan's neck. Glue the small dog whelk to one end of the neck. Glue two similar-shaped pieces of goose barnacle shell on either side of the large dog whelk as the wings and two smaller pieces for the tail. Goose barnacle shells are very light in weight and need very little support while the glue is drying.

Reeds

Materials

- Half of a small bivalve or a piece of shell as the base
- Salmon bones (one for the stem and one or two for the leaves)
- Acteon for the seedhead

Method

To make the seedhead, glue the acteon to the thinner end of one of the bones. Fix the thicker end of each bone to the base.

Water lilies

Materials

- Seven small tellin or nut valves for the petals
- Small flat winkle for the seedhead
- Small scallop valves for the leaves

Method

Place three scallop valves on the work surface and glue them together in a star-shaped leaf cluster. Glue the lily petals round the seedhead. When the glue has set, fix the completed lily on to the leaves with a spot of glue.

These lilies are designed at the same scale as the boat, the swan and the reeds. You can make larger lilies by using eight to ten tellin or white abra valves for the petals, a yellow flat winkle or a small Baltic tellin valve for the seedhead, and tiger scallop valves for the leaves.

Bridge

Materials

- Seventeen banded wedge valves for the bridge
- Thirty tusk shells; fourteen for the handrails (including four large ones at the ends) and sixteen smaller ones for the uprights

Method

Cut out a strip of cardboard the width of the bridge, bend it to form a curve and hold it in shape with a length of sticky tape (see sketch below). Assemble and glue the banded wedge valves together over the cardboard former. Leave to dry then glue the uprights and handrails on either side.

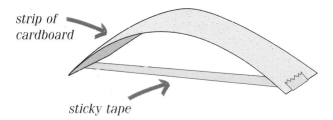

strip of cardboard

sticky tape

Boat

Materials

- Common otter shell valve for the boat
- Two banded wedge valves for seats
- Small sting winkle for the lady's body
- Netted dog whelk for the man's body
- Four small dog whelks for the upper arms
- Four ceriths for the forearms
- Two small ceriths for the man's feet
- Thirty to forty tiny ceriths for the lady's hair
- Four tusk shells for the man's legs
- Two cowries for the heads
- Two rissoas for the earrings
- Twelve thin tellin valves for the lady's skirt
- Flake of oyster shell and a piece of tusk for the man's hat
- Two sea bream bones for the oars

Method

Place the otter shell boat on the work surface and fix the two seats inside it. Assemble the lady's skirt on one of the seats then glue her upper body and head in position. Glue the man's body and then his head to the other seat – support them in position while the glue dries. Add the man's arms, legs and hat, and the lady's arms and hair. Glue on the oars, adjusting their length so that they just touch the work surface to balance the whole structure.

Goose barnacles

Goose barnacles as found on the beach.

The shell of a goose barnacle consists of five separate plates joined by ligaments. You will find them on pieces of wood and other jetsam brought in by the tide. Do not wait for the sea to clean them – they are very fragile and they are quickly destroyed if left on the beach – so take them as you find them.

To clean goose barnacles, first remove all the organic waste which comes away easily, then place them in a screw-topped jar containing 40% bleach. Be careful, because at this concentration bleach is very corrosive. Replace the lid on the jar, leave the barnacles to soak for several hours, then rinse them thoroughly. The bleach dissolves any remaining organic matter, including the ligaments, and causes the plates to separate. If you want to save a set of plates from one particular barnacle, soak them alone in a small pot to avoid getting them mixed up with others.

The snake (opposite) is made with just the long thin plate of a goose barnacle. The swan on page 12 makes use of all five plates, while the sails of the windmill on page 48 are made from eighty-eight of the large plates.

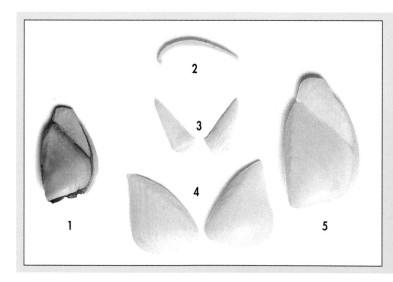

1. *Barnacle after preliminary hand cleaning*

2. *Long thin plate*

3. *Small plates*

4. *Large plates*

5. *Barnacle shell put back together after cleaning in bleach.*

The snake charmer

Materials

- Wentletrap for the upper body and two smaller ones for the lower legs
- Two dog whelks for the thighs and two smaller ones for the upper arms
- Two ceriths for the forearms
- European cowrie for the head
- Five truncated pieces of large tops (two for the turban and three for the basket)
- Long thin goose barnacle plate for the snake
- Tusk for the flute
- Tiny pheasant shell for the ruby on the turban

Method

Fix the snake charmer's head to his upper body. Assemble the thighs and the legs. Glue the apex of the upper body shell between the thighs. If the aperture of the dog whelks is too conspicuous, block it up with a piece of shell of the same colour. To make the turban, glue the two pieces of large top shells together and then fix the tiny pheasant shell ruby on the lower one. Attach the completed turban to the snake charmer's head and then glue on his arms and his flute. Make the basket with the remaining three pieces of top shell, placing the largest piece in the middle and the smallest on top. Fix the snake in the middle of the basket.

The long, thin plate of a goose barnacle is ideal for representing an upright snake.

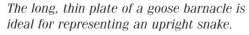

In the forest

Boletus

Materials
- Dosinia valve for the base
- Acteon for the stem
- Saddle oyster valve for the cap

Method
Glue the stem on to the base, then fix on the cap. Support everything in position with modelling clay while the glue dries. Try mounting two mushrooms on a single large base to give a more balanced composition.

Amanite

Materials
- Rock barnacle for the base
- Tusk for the stem
- Peristome for the ring
- Limpet for the cap

Method
Glue the stem vertically through the top of the rock barnacle base. Fix the ring around the stem. Place the cap on the top of the whole assembly. For larger versions make a long stem with two tusk shells – glue the narrow end of one shell inside the wide end of the other.

Lepiote

Materials
- Small piece of oyster for the base
- Tower for the stem
- Two small saddle oysters for the ring
- Dosinia valve for the cap

Method
Use a sharp pointed tool to make a hole through each small saddle oyster shell. Enlarge the holes so that half the length of the tower shell can pass through them. Glue the convex side of each shell together to complete the ring. Glue them to the stem and then the stem to the base. Finally, glue the cap to the top of the stem. If the stem shell is very pointed, make a small ring from a tusk and use this to help make a secure joint.

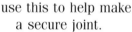

Snake

Materials
- Seven acteons for the body and head
- Two small tusks for the tongue
- Small whole banded wedge shells for the eyes

Method
Glue the body shells together, apex to aperture. Use a support to keep the snake's head up off the work surface. Finally, glue the tongue and the eyes in position.

For this snake, a netted dog whelk is used for the head. Green sea urchins and tiny black ceriths form the eyes.

Snail

Materials
- Limpet ring for the body
- Necklace shell for the shell
- Two ceriths for the horns.

Method
Glue the snail's shell to the body. Glue the thick end of the horns to the body and support them until the glue is dry.

The head of this snake is an acteon shell that has lost its apex. The two tusk shells that form the tongue are glued into the cavity.

Lactarius

Materials
- Small piece of oyster for the base
- Piece of tower shell for the stem
- Limpet and a saddle oyster valve for the cap

Method
Glue the small end of the stem on the base. Glue the limpet shell inside the saddle oyster to form the cap and then glue the cap on top of the stem.

Mycena

Materials
- Small piece of an oyster shell for the base
- Long salmon bone for the stem
- Chinese hat shell for the cap

Method
Glue the thick end of the stem to the base and the thin end inside the Chinese hat shell cap.

Goblin

Materials

- Large dog whelk for the body and four small ones for the feet and upper arms
- European cowrie for the head
- Two acteons for the thighs
- Four tusk shells for the upper legs and the forearms
- Painted top and a small slim mangelia for the hat

Method

Place all the shells for the legs on the work surface and glue them together. Note how the curve of the tusk shell is used to good effect for the lower legs. Add the feet, with the apex of each shell pointing upwards. Still working flat on the work surface, glue the head to the body – support the joint until the glue is dry. Glue the legs to the body to give the desired pose and then fix the shells for the arms in a similar manner.

Woodcutter

A classical arrangement of shells is used to create this figure. Slight changes to the relative positions of the shells can produce lots of different poses.

Materials

- Twelve limpets for the skirt
- Dog whelk for the body
- Cowrie for the head
- Piece of peristome for the headscarf
- Two dog whelks for the upper arms and two ceriths for the forearms
- Tuna bone for the walking stick
- Calcified coral for the bundle of sticks.

Method

Glue the skirt shells on top of each other. Glue the head to the body then the body to the skirt, tilting it slightly forward. Glue on the sticks one by one and then the arms. Cut the walking stick to size and glue this in position. Finally, glue on the headscarf.

Woodcutter and cart

Materials

- All the shells listed opposite for the woodcutter, minus the coral sticks
- Two small razor shell valves for the chassis of the cart
- Six tusks for the side posts
- Two straight tuna bones for the rails
- Four limpet rings (two large and two small) for the rims of the wheels
- Four grey tops for the wheel hubs
- Twenty ceriths for the spokes of the wheels
- Two tusks for the axles
- Tusk as a spacer between the front axle and the cart's body
- Large sea bream bone for the handle

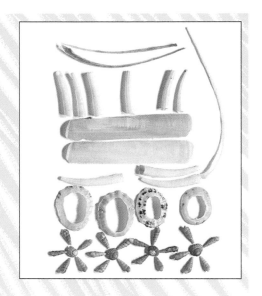

Method

Assemble the woodcutter as described opposite, but incline her slightly forward to indicate movement. Note that one of her hands is holding the handle of the cart. The wood, more substantial than in the previous model, comprises real twigs – these are placed in the completed cart. Make up each wheel. Glue five spokes in a star shape inside a limpet ring and then cover the centre joint with a wheel hub. Glue the wheels to the two axles. Glue a spacer to the axle of the small front wheels. Glue the two parts of the chassis to the axles. Add the three posts to each side of the chassis and then the tuna-bone rails. Finally, glue the thick end of the sea bream bone to the front of the cart and the other end to the lady's hand.

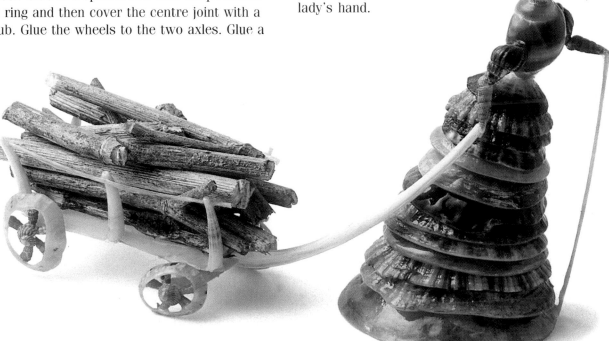

Butterflies and flowers

Small butterfly

Materials

- Two thin tellin valves for the wings
- Cerith for the body
- Salmon bone for the antennae
- Small tellin valve for the base

Method

Glue the wings on either side of the body – allow the aperture end of the cerith, which represents the head of the butterfly, to protrude slightly. Support the wings with small balls of modelling clay while the glue dries. Glue the body and wings to the base. Place a spot of glue on the head of the butterfly and, using a pair of tweezers, attach short pieces of fish bone to make the antennae.

You can also use carpet shells to make butterfly wings. These are available in a wide variety of colours and they can be used to make lots of different butterflies.

Daisy

Materials

- Five thin tellin valves (all from the same side and all the same colour) for the petals
- Flat winkle for the seedhead
- Sea bream bone for the stem
- Two tusks for the leaves
- Saddle oyster for the base

Method

Place a spot of glue on the tip of a petal, wait until it starts to set and then set it at a slight angle to the seed head. Stick on the other petals in the same way. Glue the stem and leaves to the base. Then, supporting the whole assembly, stick the completed flower head on the stem. Allow to dry for at least twelve hours.

Marigold

Materials

- Six banded wedge valves (all from the same side of the shell) for the petals
- Limpet for the seedhead
- Two tusks for the stem
- Two mussel valves for the leaves
- Banded carpet valve for the base.

Method

Arrange the petals in a star shape, concave side downwards, and glue them together. Make a long stem by gluing the two tusks together. Stick the stem to the base and then glue a leaf on each side. Glue the flower head to the stem and then cover the top with the seedhead.

Clockwise from top: a carpet shell butterfly, a marigold, a daisy and a thin tellin butterfly.

Large butterfly

Materials

- Tusk for the body
- Rough winkle for the head
- Whole carpet shell for the front wings
- Whole Baltic tellin for the rear wings
- Scallop valve for the base
- Salmon bone for the antennae

Method

Glue the apex of the rough winkle into the large end of the tusk to form the head and body. Arrange the wings on a flat surface and then start to assemble them by gluing each front wing to a back wing (the picture opposite shows the correct positioning). When the glue starts to set, attach the wings on either side of the body, supporting the assembly to maintain shape. Ensure that the head protrudes correctly. When the assembly is rigid enough to handle, glue it to the base. Finally, attach the two antennae to the head with small spots of glue.

Variations of the large butterfly

With a little imagination and the many other types of shell available, you can make a wide range of different butterflies. Here are just a few examples to inspire you.

SCALLOPS

Scallops are available in a remarkable range of colours. Sometimes, you may need to remove the small ears from the hinge of the valve; use a small saw or file to do this. In the picture opposite, the front ear of each brown scallop has been removed. The other is used as a support for the smaller orange scallops from which both ears have been removed. Choose a large cerith for the body.

OTTER SHELLS

Use the materials listed above but use otter shells instead of carpet shells for the front wings.

TROUGH SHELLS

Rayed trough shells can also be used to make butterfly wings. In the example opposite, the body is made by gluing two ceriths end to end.

MUSSELS

Mussel valves have a wonderful shape, exactly right for butterfly wings. Use pairs of valves from the same mussel to achieve symmetrical wings. Select a large mussel for the front wings and one about half the size for the rear wings. Use a large cerith for the body.

Clockwise from top left: mussels; otter shells and tellins; scallops; carpet shells and Baltic tellins; rayed trough shells.

Animals

Donkey

Materials

- Carpet shell for the body
- Four tower shells for the legs
- Baltic tellin for the neck
- Two tusks and a small dog whelk for the tail
- Three banded wedges for the head and ears
- Two dwarf winkles for the eyes

Method

Glue the two valves of the banded wedges, the Baltic tellin and the carpet shell together. Push the two tusks into each other to make the tail and then glue the dog whelk to the end of the tail. Refer to the picture below when gluing the body, the neck, the head and the ears together. Support the components in position while the glue dries. When the assembly is dry, place the body on a small stem of modelling clay and then glue on the legs, the tail and finally the eyes. Leave the supports in place for at least twelve hours.

Horse

Materials

- Three whelks for the body
- Five wentletraps (four for the legs and one for the tail)
- Four small dog whelks for the legs and two smaller ones for the ears
- Four grey tops for the hooves
- Banded wedge for the head and a tower shell for the neck
- Thirty to sixty ceriths for the mane

Method

Glue two whelks together, aperture to aperture, to start the body, then glue the aperture of the third whelk on one end so that its apex starts to form the horse's neck. Glue the tower shell, apex turned upwards, over the third whelk. Glue the tail on the other end of the body. Glue the two banded wedge valves together to make the head and then glue the head to the neck. Create the mane by gluing the tiny ceriths along the sides and back of the neck and then glue on the ears.

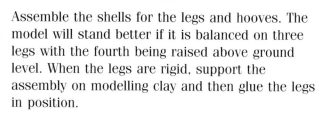

Assemble the shells for the legs and hooves. The model will stand better if it is balanced on three legs with the fourth being raised above ground level. When the legs are rigid, support the assembly on modelling clay and then glue the legs in position.

Spider

Materials

- Two large winkles for the body and two small ones for the labial feelers
- Sixteen tusks for the legs and two smaller ones for the maxillary feelers
- Three tiny nut valves
- Two small green sea urchins for the eyes

Method

Glue the two large winkles together, end to end, with both apertures face down. Assemble two tusks for each of the legs, setting each pair at a different angle. Support the body up off the work surface and then glue on the legs. Decorate the rear of the body with tiny nut valves then glue on the feelers and eyes.

In order to make your models more lifelike, refer to illustrations and photographs, then adapt them to fit the shape of your shells. Do not be afraid of exaggeration – use your imagination.

Rat

Materials

- Dog whelk for the body
- Small dog whelk for the head, four smaller ones for the legs, two very small ones for the ears and two tiny ones for the eyes
- Two tusks for the tail

Method

Place the body shell, aperture face down, on the work surface. Glue the legs to the body – the front ones upright and the rear ones flat. Join the two tusks together and then glue the tail on the body. Fix the aperture of the head shell over the apex of the body shell and then add the ears and eyes.

Mouse

Materials

- Dog whelk for the body
- Two small dog whelks for the feet
- Winkle for the head
- Salmon bone for the whiskers
- Two small green sea urchins for the eyes
- Two Chinese hats for the ears
- Two tusks for the tail

Method

Assemble the components as described for the rat, but omit the rear legs. Complete the model by gluing on the ears, eyes and whiskers.

It is easier to balance models of dogs if they are in a sitting pose, so there are three points of contact on the work surface.

Poodle

Materials

- Three large dog whelks for the body and head, four average size ones for the legs and three small ones for the ears and tail

- Truncated grey top for the collar

Method

Glue the two body shells together then glue the front legs to the body so that the model is balanced on three points. Support the model and then glue on the rear legs, the tail, the collar, the head and, finally, the ears.

Dachshund

Materials

- Two tusks – the wide end of a large one for the body, and the thin end of a small one for the tail

- Two ceriths (half the size of the body) for the front legs, two smaller ones for the rear legs and two or three tiny ones for the collar

- Two small whole banded wedges for the head and ears

Method

Glue two banded wedge valves together for the head. Glue the legs to the body, positioning the front ones in a near vertical position and the rear ones horizontal to the work surface. Glue on the tail. Attach the head, using a support while the glue dries. Add the ears by gluing the umbo of each shell against the tusk. Make the collar by placing small ceriths between the head and body.

Squid

Materials

- Dog whelk for the body

- Two necklace shells for the head

- Sixteen tusks for the tentacles

Method

Assemble pairs of tusks to form long tentacles and then glue them under the apex of the body. Glue the two eyes in position, with the tips of the shells pointing outwards.

This model of a crocodile uses long flat pieces of oyster shell which would often be discarded.

Crocodile

Materials

- Two flat oyster valves for the head, one each for the body and tail
- Eight large dog whelks for the legs and fourteen small ones for the teeth
- Two banded wedge valves and two ceriths for the eyes.

Method

Make the crocodile's head by gluing two flat valves together at one end, with the pearly sides facing each other. Glue the ceriths on the banded wedge valves to make the eyes, then glue them on the head. Glue the lower teeth in position then, when they are dry, turn the head over and glue the upper teeth in position. Glue the head to the body and then add the tail. Finally, glue the legs together and attach them to the body.

Pelican

The pelican's body is a whelk, whose balance is ensured by three points of support: its own rear end and the two valves of the cockle.

Materials

- Whelk for the body
- Whole cockle for the legs
- Two dog whelks for the neck
- Oyster valve for the top of the head and slipper limpet for the lower part
- Two rough winkles for the eyes

Method

Glue the legs together, hinge to hinge. Glue the body on the legs so that the tip of its aperture rests on the work surface. Attach the neck to the body – glue one dog whelk in a horizontal position, with its apex pointing to the rear and its aperture upwards. When the glue is dry, place the apex of a second shell in the aperture of the first, tilting it slightly backwards. Glue the oyster valve for the top of the head so that it is straddling the edge of the slipper limpet, with its more pointed end overlapping so that it fits into the aperture at the top of the neck. Finally, glue on the eyes.

Mythical creatures

Shells can be used to create a whole host of wild and wondrous creatures . . .

Whelkinosaurus

Materials

- Whelk with a broken apex for the body
- Eight tusks for the neck and tail
- Small dog whelk for the head
- Cockle for the legs

Method

Assemble six tusks for the neck and two for the tail. Glue the two cockle valves together, hinge to hinge, to make the feet and then glue the body in position. Glue the head to the neck. When this assembly is rigid, glue it to the body, using supports to prop the neck in the required position. Leave the model to dry for at least twelve hours.

Chinese dragon

Materials

- Seven dog whelks for the body
- Whole oyster for the head

- Clump of rock barnacles for the crest
- Four small dog whelks for the teeth
- Two rough winkles for the eyes
- Two whole scallops for the wings
- Sting winkle and three tusks for the tail

Sea serpent

Materials

- Eleven large whelks, decreasing in size, and five dog whelks for the body
- Oyster shell for the head
- Assorted shells to decorate the body and the head (cockles, pelican's foot shells, Queen scallops, columellas, rock barnacles)

Method

Assemble and secure the whelks, starting with the largest, with the apex of each glued inside the aperture of the previous shell. Add five dog whelks at the tail end. Embellish the body with a few shells of your choice. On the model in the photograph, the back flippers are made from cockle valves and a pelican's foot shell represents the dorsal flipper. On the neck, another pelican's foot shell has been placed between two Queen scallop valves, which form the magnificent pectoral flippers. The head is created with a half-opened oyster shell and the teeth are made from small dog whelks. A small columella forms the tongue and rock barnacles are used for the eyes.

Method

Make the head in the same way as the crocodile on page 27. Assemble the body and tail, placing the shells with their apertures face down in a flat, wavy line. Use a support to glue the head to the body and then create a crest on the head with the rock barnacles. Finally, add the wings to the body as shown in the picture opposite.

Clockwise from top left: sea serpent, whelkinosaurus and Chinese dragon.

Comical characters

Oyster shells can be found in an enormous variety of shapes, colours and sizes, and it is also possible to modify their shape. They are perfect for making a wide range of comical figures. Try varying attributes such as hair and eyes, add bizarre hats or whatever else sparks your imagination. The gluing tricks included below are particularly relevant to the models on this page, but they will also come in useful for other shell compositions.

Mr C Urchin

Materials

- A whelk for the body
- A whole mussel and a limpet for the feet
- A limpet ring for the neck
- A whole oyster for the mouth
- Two flat winkles for the eyes
- A sea urchin test for the hat

Method

Assemble the body to the feet with the aid of a limpet (see gluing trick No. 2). Fix the head to the body using a thin limpet ring (see gluing trick No. 1). Fix the mouth in the open position and glue on the eyes. Support the model while the glue dries. Finally, glue on the hat.

Mr L Cockle

As indicated by his name, this figure's hat is made from a large cockle valve. The eyes are made from two small necklace shells. The whelk used for the body had suffered from the effects of erosion and had lost its apex, so it was not necessary to use gluing trick No. 2.

Mr Star Fish

Grey tops make up the eyes of this little chap. The apex of each shell is turned towards one another to give the character an amiable squint which is rather touching. His body is made with the same types of shells as Mr C Urchin and he is finished star fish crazy hair.

GLUING TRICKS

1. Instead of gluing a shell directly on to the sharp pointed apex of a whelk (or other gastropod), use a limpet with a large hole at the top as a joining aid. Glue the upturned limpet over the apex of the whelk to form a firm support for the next shell, even if it is a heavy one.

2. Sometimes, it can prove difficult to glue a body on to feet made up of two valves from a cockle, mussel, banded wedge, etc, set hinge to hinge. Again, the limpet shell can be used to good effect. Glue an upturned limpet to the feet with its apex wedged between them. It is then possible to glue another shell into the hollow without any risk of slippage.

Clockwise from top: Mr Star Fish; Mr C Urchin; Mr L Cockle

Aeroplanes

Razor shells can be glued together to make an aeroplane. It is easy to do – here are three different models based on the same technique.

Basic aeroplane

Materials

- Razor valve for the fuselage, a longer one for the front wings and a smaller one for the rear wing
- Whole thick trough for the tailplane
- Two banded wedge valves for the propeller
- Two limpet rings for the wheels

Method

Place the front and rear wings parallel to each other, hollow side upwards then glue the fuselage, also hollow side up, on top of the wings. Glue the wheels to the front wings, either side of the fuselage. Place the two propellers on the work surface, one with the hollow side down and glue them together, end to end, with a slight overlap. Turn the fuselage right way up and glue the tailplane on to the rear wing, supporting it on both sides while the glue dries. Finally, glue the propeller to the front of the fuselage.

Biplane

Materials

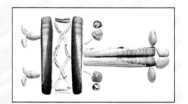

- Whole razor shell for the fuselage and two longer valves for the front wings
- Two large banded wedge valves for the rear wings and four smaller valves (all from the same side of the shell) for the propellers
- Small thick trough shell for the tailplane
- Two bulla shells for the engines
- Two truncated grey tops for the wheels
- Two small saddle oysters for the mudguards
- Four thick tusks for the front wing supports and about twenty-eight thin tusks for the wire stays and wheel supports

Method

Glue the two valves for the fuselage together then the two valves for the tailplane. Place the lower front wing, hollow side down, on the work surface and glue a wing support in each corner. Leave to dry. Lay the two valves for the rear wing, hollow side down, so their ventral edges align and glue them together, end to end. Glue the tailplane to the rear wing. Glue pairs of propeller shells together, end to end. Assemble the wheels by gluing a truncated grey top into the hollow part of a saddle oyster, then fixing a short length of tusk to the top of the mudguard. Leave to dry. Glue the upper front wing to the four supports on the lower wing, and the fuselage to the centre of it. Push three tusks into each other to form a wire stay. Make three more wire stays. Trim each stay with a pair of pincers to fit the wings, as shown in the picture opposite, and then glue them in position. Glue the propellers to the engines and then glue the engines to the wing. Glue the rear wing and tailplane to the fuselage. Support the fuselage above the work surface and glue the completed wheel assemblies to the wing.

Top to bottom:
biplane, basic aeroplane
and monoplane.

Monoplane

Materials

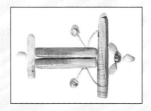

- Whole razor shell for the fuselage, a longer valve for the front wing and a smaller one for the rear wing
- Small thick trough valve for the tailplane
- Three banded wedge valves (all from the same side) for the propeller
- Grey top for the propeller hub and two truncated grey tops for the wheels
- Two tusks for the wing struts and two smaller ones for the wheel struts

Method

Glue the two valves for the fuselage together. Place the front and rear wings parallel to each other, hollow side up. Glue the fuselage to the wings, support in position and leave to dry. Assemble the propellers – lay three valves, hollow side down, on the work surface and glue them together, end to end. Glue the hub in the middle of the propeller assembly. Glue the wing struts to the fuselage and wing, with the wide end attached slightly above the bottom of the fuselage. Glue the wheel struts to the fuselage and wing struts, support them at an appropriate angle and leave to dry. Glue the wheels to the wheel struts. When the model is rigid, turn it over, glue the tailplane to the rear wing and support it on either side. Finally, glue the propeller assembly to the fuselage.

Setting the scene

Shells can be used to create a range of different figures . . . but what really brings them to life is a setting. Here are a variety of props that are very simple to make. Most of the characters on these two pages are made from dog whelks.

Robinson Crusoe

The leaves of this palm tree are made from eleven banded wedge valves. To make them, follow the instructions for the marigold on page 20.

Lute player

The lute is a worn sting winkle with a wentletrap on the end. The strings are made of sewing thread, but you could also use fine fish bones. The feet are flat winkles. The base is a limpet set on an oyster, but a large flattish limpet would do just as well.

Swordsmen

The swords are made from tuna bones. A base is essential for this model so that the characters can be posed correctly. Here they are mounted on a large flat stone.

Four men on a bench

The bench is made up of two razor valves (one for the seat, the other for the backrest). The bench is supported on two limpets. The newspaper is made of paper, but you could equally well use a small piece of shell.

Card players

The table is a large pebble supported on a piece of calcified coral. The seats are limpets.

The figures shown on these pages do incorporate ceriths, tusks, cowries and cone shells.

Tyrolean

The table top is a piece of glass polished by the sea; its leg a columella set on top of the remains of a dog whelk. The man's legs are tusks fixed to pieces of wentletrap, and his hat is a small rock barnacle decorated with a tiny duck feather.

Dice players

The table is a flat pebble supported on a tower shell. The dice are large grains of sand. In this model, the dice player's legs are made up of two wentletraps.

Tourist

The carafe is a piece of tusk and the glass a tiny cerith. The base is not essential.

Englishman

The man's head is an acteon and his hat is a peristome with a small necklace shell on top. His thighs are wentletraps, his boots are tusks and his feet small nassas. The table is a flat pebble supported on a tower shell. The glass is a small acteon and the carafe is a piece of tusk with small peristome handles.

The dice players and the tourist sit on simple seats made from limpets, while the Tyrolean and the Englishman sit on more elaborate chairs. The frame of each chair is made from tusks, the seat is a small queen scallop, and the backrest is a limpet ring.

Impressionist painter

Four tower shells support the easel. The palette is a banded wedge valve. Tiny ceriths are used to create the artist's hair and the feet. A cowrie create his portly body shape and worm shells are used for his legs.

Gardeners

The hat of the gardener on the left is a limpet ring with a small necklace shell on top. The rose on the watering can is a small Chinese hat shell. The spade for the gardener on the right is a small saddle oyster valve.

Artist

The artist's skirt is made from three oyster valves. Use ones that have not worn too much by the sea, so that they still retain some decorative patterns. Her brush is a small fish bone with a tiny pheasant shell on the tip, and the palette is a flat piece of oyster shell.

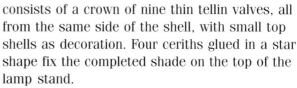

Reading at a table

The lady reading her book is sitting next to a table made by gluing a flat pebble to three tusks.

The base of the lamp stand is a Chinese hat and the column is a pair of acteons separated by a tiny, but whole cockle. The lampshade consists of a crown of nine thin tellin valves, all from the same side of the shell, with small top shells as decoration. Four ceriths glued in a star shape fix the completed shade on the top of the lamp stand.

Two scallop valves, glued together at right angles, hinge to hinge, form the seat and backrest of the lady's chair. Approximately forty tiny black ceriths form her hair, her earrings are rissoa shells and her book is a small piece of razor shell.

Photographer

The camera (a rock barnacle with a small grey top for the lens) is fixed on a tripod made up of three sea bream bones and a small painted top shell.

Sailors

These dinghies are mussel valves glued on oyster valve bases. Small pieces of razor shell form the seat and large fish bones create the mast and rigging. The sails are large angel wing valves. The flag on top of one of the masts is part of a worm shell.

Cross-country skier

Each ski is made by overlapping two small razor shell valves. Fish bones and tiny peristomes are used for the ski poles. The skier's legs are tusks and wentletraps, and his hat is a small Chinese hat shell. Three-point balance is provided by the right-hand ski pole, the flat of the left-hand ski and the tip of the right-hand one.

Cyclist

The wheels are made from limpet rings and small ceriths. The wheel hubs are purple top shells with their tips facing inwards. The forks are two tusks joined together by a small banded wedge. The frame and handlebars consist of tusk shells, some of which are glued together, thick end to thick end. The handlebar drops are two pieces of peristome. A tiny purple top shell, apex pointing outwards, is used as the chain wheel. The chain is two pieces of fish bone. A banded wedge valve forms the saddle and small ceriths create the pedals. The cyclist's helmet is a small peristome surmounted by a small Chinese hat shell.

A real regatta! The ripples on the oyster shell bases create a realistic impression of water.

Fantasy world

Troll

The body is made of a large dog whelk, apex pointing upwards and the aperture at the front of the figure. The thighs are small dog whelks, the legs small nassas, the feet tiny gastropods, the arms sting winkles and the forearms ceriths. An extended rock barnacle columella represents the neck. A yellow flat winkle, aperture facing forwards, makes a nice shiny skull. The mouth, glued between the neck and the head, is a rock barnacle. The eyes are two small green sea urchins, one of which fills up the aperture of the winkle. The ears are two rissoas.

Warrior

The body is a cowrie, the legs are edible winkles, the feet are small top shells, the arms are brown rough winkles, and the forearms are nassas. The head is a whole oyster shell with four ceriths as teeth. One of the ears is an oddly-shaped oyster shell, the other is a small nassa. The warrior's shield is a black valve from a tiger scallop shell, decorated with a rissoa and a peristome. The axe head is a piece of limpet. The axe handle rests on the ground to balance the figure.

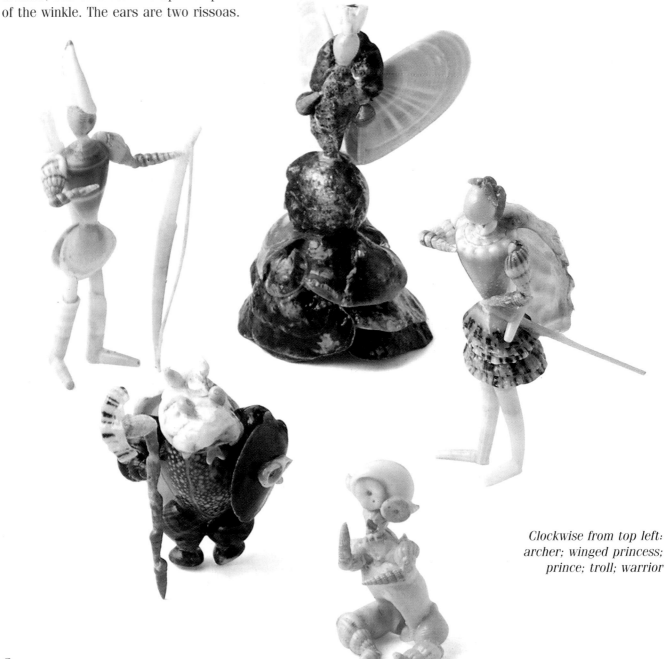

Clockwise from top left: archer; winged princess; prince; troll; warrior

Coat of arms

Five tusks frame the remains of a flat, polished oyster shell and form the shield. Fleurs-de-lis, made of ceriths, are separated by a motif made from small scallop valves joined together by a piece of razor shell.

Winged princess

Twelve convex saddle oyster valves form the skirt, and another, slightly worn, valve forms the collar. The upper body is a sting winkle, the arms are small dog whelks and the forearms are short pieces of tusk. The head, a cowrie shell, is topped with a rock barnacle. Two banded wedge valves (the wings) complete the model.

Archer

The body is a colourful cone shell. Two Baltic tellin valves, glued only on the top edge, make up the breeches. Tusks form the legs and boots. The arms are small nassas, the forearms are ceriths and the head is a cowrie shell. The hat is a crab claw, the quiver a tusk and the arrows are salmon bones. The bow consists of two tusks glued thick end to thick end and the bowstring is a fishbone.

Prince

This character has much in common with the archer – the body, arms, legs and head are identical. The kilt is made of five similar limpets. The collar is a peristome. Tiny dog whelks represent the hair – three are glued to the back of the head and one on either side of the top. The cloak is a convex oyster valve. The sword is made from a fishbone and two pieces of tusk – one for the handle, the other for the hilt.

King

The backrest of the throne is a large razor valve. A small flat oyster valve seat is glued to the backrest, one-third up from the base. A cone shell (which forms the body) is glued by its apex on to the seat. Three large mussel valves make up the bulk of the king's robe, with smaller ones glued on the inside to fill any gaps. The cloak (two mussel valves) is glued between the body and the backrest of the chair. The arms are nassas, the forearms tower shells, the head a cowrie. The eyes and the chain are peristomes. The pendant on the chain is a pea sea urchin pendant. The moustache is made with two small crab claws. The collar is a piece of rock barnacle and an upturned whole rock barnacle forms the crown.

Buildings

Cottage

Materials

- About two hundred mussel valves for the walls
- About thirty razor valves (three for the door frame, the rest for the roof)
- Gaper shell valve for the door, four ceriths for the hinges and a flat winkle for the door knob
- Twenty tusks for the windows, and sixteen pink, thin tellin valves for the curtains
- Six banded wedge valves (two for the doorstep and one for each window sill)

Dimensions

Front: 20cm (8in) wide x 8cm (3in) high

Left side: 12cm (4¾in) wide x 16.5cm (6½in) to top of chimney

Right side: 12cm (4¾in) wide x 15cm (6in) to top of the roof

Windows (4): 3cm (1¼in) wide x 3.5cm (1½in) high, 3cm (1¼in) above ground level

Door: 3cm (1¼in) wide x 5.5cm (2¼in) high

Method

The four sides of the cottage must be assembled on a flat work surface. Use the dimensions given above to draw a full-size template of each side and then assemble the shells on the templates.

Start by building the four windows – there are two at the front and two at the rear. Form the window frames and window sills from three tusks and a banded wedge valve. Create the window panes with two more tusks glued as a cross to each window frame. Glue the curtains behind the frame, with their colourful, convex sides pointing outwards.

Now build the walls using mussel valves as bricks. Build one wall with right-hand-side valves and the other one with left-hand-side valves. Assemble a row of valves, hollow side flat on the work surface, with the wide end of one valve covering the tip of

It is also possible to build the cottage in much the same way as a real house, working round and upwards. The valves are placed as interconnecting bricks, with their hollow side face down. You will need a lot more shells but the walls will be thicker and the house more solid. In the example shown here, the door and window frames are decorated with banded wedge valves.

the roof on the former and glue them together with razor shell ridge tiles. Take care not to allow any glue to seep on to the former. When the roof is rigid, slide it off the former and then glue it on to the walls.

cardboard former folded to correct roof pitch

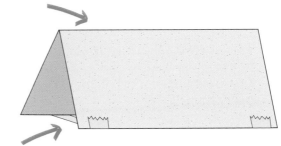

sticky tape

Leave the model to dry for twenty-four hours, then turn the cottage upside down and block up the remaining large gaps with small mussel valves.

This picture shows the inside of the cottage. Wait until the glue is really dry before turning it over and filling any holes with small mussel valves.

the previous one. Set a second row on top, with the tips pointing in the opposite direction.

Continue gluing more rows of bricks until you reach the required height. When the sides are finished, glue in the windows and then assemble the door and its fittings. When all the walls are set solid, assemble them together using whole mussels on the inside corners to add strength to the construction and to blocks up any gaps.

Make each side of the roof separately, gluing razor valves side by side. Remember to place short valves at the chimney ends. It is best to use a cardboard former when assembling the roof. Make the former longer than the roof itself so you can handle it easily. Fold the cardboard to create the correct roof pitch and hold it in shape with sticky tape (see sketch). Place the two assembled sides of

Lighthouse

Materials

- Piece of razor shell and three tusks for the doorframe
- Six small tusks for the door and a dwarf winkle for the doorknob
- Thirty tusks for the windows
- About one hundred and twenty small dog whelks for the walls
- Five or six pieces of calcified coral (or tusks), a dozen yellow flat winkles, seven tusks, seven banded wedge valves, one saddle oyster, a small grey top and a fish bone for the lantern.
- Six ceriths for the seagull
- Twelve large cockle valves (preferably black) for the small island
- Twelve tusks, sixteen ceriths and a number of grey tops for the steps

Dimensions

Height of tower (without aerial): 17.5cm (7in)

Diameter of the tower: 5.5cm (2¼in)

Method

The walls of this lighthouse must be built vertically. However, the doors and windows are assembled on a flat surface and glued to the building during its construction.

Make the door frame by gluing two tusks, tips upward, to the ends of a short razor shell and then gluing another tusk across the top. Fill the bottom of the door with four small tusks glued head to foot and create window panes in the upper half with two tusks arranged as a cross. Glue on the knob.

Next make the windows – there are two windows above the door and three on the other side of the lighthouse. Build each window frame with four tusks, glued with the large aperture of one against the tip of the next. Glue two more tusks in a cross shape to form the window panes.

Now build the tower using the dog whelks; on this model there are thirteen rows of shells with six to eight shells in each row. Glue the shells horizontally, with the apex of one against the aperture of the next. Fit the doors and windows as you proceed. Fill in any gaps with small shells.

Use the pieces of calcified coral (or tusks) to form a base ring for the lamp assembly. Make it slightly larger in diameter than the top of the tower. Make a top ring, the same size as the base ring, using flat winkles. Join the two rings together with the six tusks, gluing them vertically with their narrow ends upward. Glue banded wedge valves, hollow side outwards, on the inside of the lamp assembly between pairs of tusks. Crown the whole structure with the saddle oyster and a grey top. Glue on a fishbone aerial and complete this part of the model with a seagull made from ceriths. Glue the completed lamp assembly to the tower.

Glue three cockle valves together vertically to form a solid base for the lighthouse. Glue the tower on top and support it with modelling clay until the glue is dry. When the structure is solid, arrange the remaining cockle valves to form the rocky island. Assemble the steps with tusks, the handrail with ceriths and then complete the model with some grey top boulders on each side of the steps.

The dog whelks used for the walls are arranged randomly to accentuate the rustic character of the structure. The whiteness of the tusks, the pearly sheen of the banded wedges and the saddle oyster, and the brightness of the yellow flat winkles give the lamp assembly a certain luminosity.

Castle wall

This section of wall can be used as a background for many of the characters shown in this book. You can also use this very simple building method to make complete buildings on to which you can assemble doors, windows and other decoration of your choice.

Materials

- Approximately one hundred and sixty netted dog whelks
- Oyster valve, two crab claws and two tiny pheasant shells for the hunting trophy.

Method

Build the wall on a flat surface, with the shell apertures face down. Arrange the first row of shells in a straight line, close together and at an angle that allows a slight overlap. For the next row stagger the shells so that they interconnect as with normal brickwork. Use broken or small shells to create square ends to the walls. Start to build the archway by assembling the shells in much the same way. Continue adding more rows of shells until the model is at the required height. Build another small section of wall and glue this at right angles to the main wall to provide balance. Fill in any gaps in the corner and around the door with small or broken shells.

The hunting trophy mounted on this wall is an oyster shell which was chosen for its shape. Two crab claws represent the horns and two pheasant shells the eyes.

Windmill

Materials

- Approximately one hundred and eighty tellin valves for the walls
- Limpet shell and about seventy variegated scallop valves for the roof and dormer window
- Approximately eighty-eight large goose barnacle plates, twelve razor valves and two top shells for the sails
- Three razor valves for the doorframe, a gaper valve for the door, four ceriths for the hinges and a small flat winkle for the handle
- Five tusks for each window frame, a small razor valve for the sill and four small saddle oyster valves (or one large one) for the window panes
- Tusk and banded wedge valve for the flagpole and flag
- Two oyster valves and ten banded wedge valves for the steps
- Four large razor shells for the post

Dimensions

Walls: 22cm (8¾in) high x 16cm (6¼in) diameter

Roof: 13cm (5in) high

Windows: 2cm (¾in) wide x 3cm (1¼in) high

Door: 5cm (2in) wide x 7cm (2¾in) high

Steps: 2.5cm (1in) high

Sail: 18cm (7in) long x 4cm (1½in) wide

Method

Decide on the number of windows that you want and then build them and the door on a flat surface as described on pages 42 and 43. Cut a 16cm (6¼in) diameter, corrugated cardboard template for the windmill's base. Glue a row of tellin valves vertically, around the edge of the template. Tellin valves are thin and lightweight, hence rather fragile, but their relative flatness makes them ideal for constructing walls. They are symmetrical in shape so you can use a mixture of left- and right-hand valves. Continue to add further rows, over-lapping and staggering the shells to fill any gaps. Remember to leave a space for the door. The model shown on page 49 is made up of twelve rows of fifteen valves. Although tellin valves are light-weight, you may find it helpful to support them with strips of cardboard or pieces of wood. As the wall gets taller, check that it remains vertical and remember to leave openings for the windows. Windows can be inserted as you build the walls or added when the walls are complete. Do not worry about any small gaps which may appear between the valves or around the openings – these can be filled with small valves glued on the inside later.

Cut a template for the roof, sized as shown in the diagram, then glue the template into a cone shape. Place the template on top of the mill to check its fit and make any necessary adjustments. Cut a hole, slightly larger than the diameter of the cone template, in a piece of corrugated cardboard and set the template in the hole. Build the roof on the template, overlapping scallop valves as shown

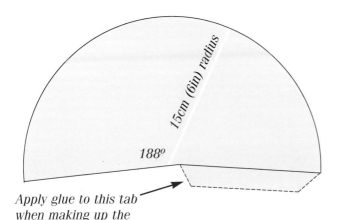

15cm (6in) radius

188°

Apply glue to this tab when making up the conical roof template.

Place the conical roof template in a circular hole cut out of thick corrugated cardboard. The resultant lip supports the first row of valves. Use strips of cardboard to support subsequent rows of shells.

above (it is rarely necessary to break off the ears of the scallops). Support the valves with strips of cardboard. Remember to leave space for the dormer window. Crown the top of the roof with a limpet.

Build the axle for the sails using four razor valves each equal in length to the diameter of the mill.

The axle for the sails is made of four razor valves assembled in the shape of a cylinder.

Glue them together, side by side, to form a cylindrical shape as shown above. Glue a top shell, aperture outwards, into one end of the axle. Slide the axle through the roof opening and glue it in position. Add a few scallop valves around this opening or build a small dormer window.

Separate the goose barnacle plates for the sails into groups – use the right-hand plates for two opposite sails and the left-hand plates for the other two. Work on a flat surface and glue pairs of plates

together, hollow side downwards, to create each sail. Glue two razor valves together, apertures face down, overlapping them to form a sail support 5cm (2in) longer than the sail. Glue a sail on the end of the sail support. Build three similar sails. Glue the four sail supports together and cover the join with a top shell. Prop the mill on the working surface with its axle pointing upwards. Temporarily place the completed sail assembly on the axle and prop each sail with a large support. Rotate the sails until you are happy with their position and then glue them on to the top shell in the end of the axle.

When the whole structure is set solid, turn the windmill back on its base. Build the steps with banded wedge valves and place an oyster valve on each side of them. Glue the flag to the flag pole and set it on the top of the roof. Glue four large razor valves together to form the post which the miller uses to turn the sails into the wind – this can be glued to the underside of the roof, diametrically opposite the sail assembly. However, to make it easier to carry the model, the post can be left loose and glued on when it has been placed in its display position.

This picture shows a side view of the windmill with the sails mounted on their axle. It also shows the construction of the dormer window over the axle.

The natural colour of the shells used to make this windmill are ideal for depicting such a rustic building.

Tower

Materials

- Approximately four hundred dog whelks for the walls
- Three razor valves for the floor of the tower
- Five tusks for the arch window
- Ten ceriths for the flag pole and a piece of shell for the flag

Dimensions

Tower: 20.5cm (8in) high x 8.5cm (3¼in) diameter

Method

Build the walls with dog whelks, gluing them together so that the aperture of one covers the apex of the previous one. This method of construction gives the tower a more rustic character than the castle wall shown on page 46. The battlements are also dog whelks glued, apexes downwards, on to the outside of the walls. Assemble the tusks in the shape of an arch, and then glue the arch in the wall as required. Glue a floor made from razor shells three rows from the top of the tower. Make the flag pole by gluing the ceriths apex to aperture.

Rapunzel

Materials

- Sting winkle for the body
- Cowrie for the head
- Six different sizes of slipper limpet for the skirt
- Two small dog whelks for the arms and two ceriths for the forearms
- Tower for the hat and three small pieces of tusk for the veil

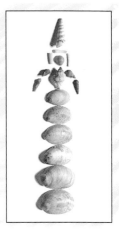

Method

Glue the head on the tip of the body – you may find it easier to glue a small collar (a short piece of tusk) between the head and body (see also page 30). Assemble the six shells for the skirt on top of each other, starting with the largest shell face down on the work surface. When the skirt is rigid, glue the aperture of the body shell on top. If you do not want to prop the model while the glue dries, lay it flat on the work surface. Glue the arms and forearms together at suitable angles and then glue them to the body. Glue the hat on the head and then glue the three pieces of the veil round the head.

This picture shows another view of the tower and its ramparts, with Rapunzel standing on the top floor.

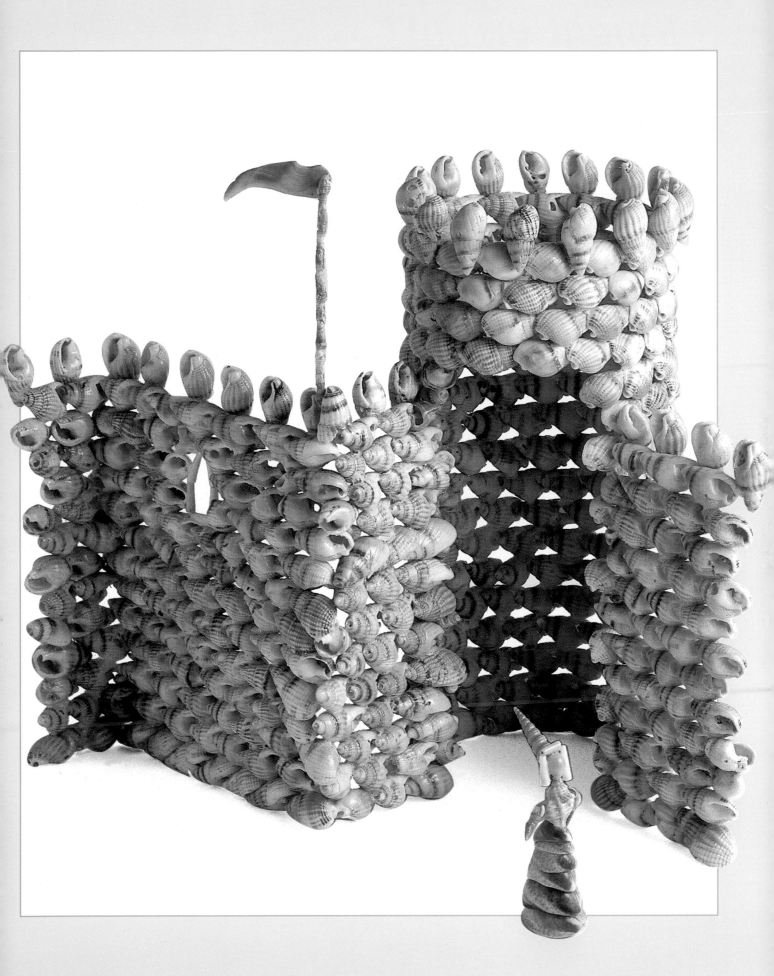

Knight errant

Don Quixote

Glue the belt on to the stomach and the stomach to the saddle. Make each leg by pushing two tusks together and gluing a cerith at the narrow end. Glue a leg to each side of the belt and attach a foot in each stirrup. Glue the tip of the body to the centre of the belt. Assemble and glue the arms – one arm points downwards to carry the shield, the other upwards to hold the lance. Glue the neck and head together, placing the aperture of the nassa over the top of the tusk. Add the eyes, the nose and the moustache. The chin and goatee beard are portrayed by the tip of the nassa. Fix the helmet to the top of the head: here we have used a large, flat remnant of a gastropod. Glue a cerith across the fish bone sword to represent its hilt.

Materials

- Wentletrap for the upper body, a tusk for the neck, a truncated grey top for the stomach and a peristome for the belt
- Four tusks for the legs and two ceriths for the feet
- Two small dog whelks for the upper arms and two ceriths for the forearms
- Nassa for the head, two dwarf winkles for the eyes, a cerith for the nose and two very small ones (or two rissoas) for the moustache
- The remains of a spherical gastropod for the helmet, a saddle oyster valve for the shield, a fish bone and a cerith for the sword, and fourteen ceriths and a tusk for the lance

Rossinante

Don Quixote's horse is similar to the one on page 24, but large dog whelks are used for the body. The saddle is made up of three pieces of shell. Attach the reins (two fish bones) to the pommel and to the horse's mouth. Make the stirrups with fish bones and peristomes, then fix them either side of the saddle. The horse's ceremonial collar consists of twenty-four ceriths glued to the body with their apexes pointing inwards. Four more ceriths, glued side by side, attach it to the saddle.

Don Quixote, astride his horse Rossinante, and his servant, Sancho Panza riding on a humble donkey.

Sancho Panza

Materials

- Acteon for the upper body
- Cowrie for the head
- Two nassas for the thighs, two smaller ones for the feet and two wentletraps for the calves
- Two small nassas for the arms and two ceriths for the forearms
- Peristome and a small necklace shell for the hat, and some fragments of edible winkles for the saddle bag

Method

Fix the head to the body (see page 30). Glue the body on the donkey's back. Assemble the legs and glue them to the body. Assemble and glue on the arms. Finally, add the hat and the saddle bag.

Donkey

The donkey is very similar to the one on page 24, but it has a thick trough shell for the neck (instead of a Baltic tellin), just one banded wedge valve for each ear and one single tusk as the tail. Each leg is made of a nassa glued to the body, followed by a

small wentletrap and a grey top for the hoof. Prepare the four legs separately, and then fix them to the body before the glue has completely set so you can adjust their position.

Little Red Riding Hood

The wolf's neck is a very worn whelk. Two flat oyster valves represent the jaws. The teeth are ceriths, with two large crab claws for the canines. Between them, the tongue is a thin piece of oyster shell, polished by the sea. The eyes are cylinder shells, and the remnants of two black nassas are used for the ears. The body is a large cone shell, four large netted dog whelks make up the arms, and three more are used for the tail. Nine tusks form the braces, with a tiny peristome joining them at the back and three green sea urchins attaching

them to the trousers (which are the remnants of two whelks). The feet are two banded wedge valves.

Most of Little Red Riding Hood is made from orange scallop valves. A small valve represents her hat and a larger one her cloak. Use eighteen or so valves for her skirt – build a cone with five valves, assemble a second row of valves underneath the first one and then glue a single valve, convex side upwards, inside the skirt to support the legs. A tusk shell forms each leg, the narrow end of which is glued into a cerith shell foot. The arms are nassas and ceriths, the upper body a cone shell, the head a cowrie and the neck a peristome. The basket is a slipper limpet, with a peristome for a handle – inside, it contains a flat winkle and a green sea urchin.

Scene 2

HORRIBLE ENCOUNTER ON THE HEATH

Here, the shells chosen for the wolf are nearly all black ones. The head is different from that of the wolf in Scene 1. The eyes are fairly large pheasant shells, the ears are whole netted dog whelks, and the body is a whole whelk glued to the remains of another one whose aperture is covered by a cockle.

In this scene, Little Red Riding Hood's upper body is a sting winkle and her hood is made of two purple-tinted saddle oyster valves. Seventeen limpets, heaped on top of each other, make up her skirt. The whole figure is inclined backwards to express horror.

USING BASES

Shell models appear more elegant without a base. However, if a model does not balance naturally, a base must be used – choose a base carefully so that it complements the subject, fits in with the structure or fades into the background.

THREE-POINT-SUPPORT RULE

Three support points provide stability to a model, and the greater the distance between the points, the more effective they are. If a model needs more than three points of contact, start by balancing the model on three, wait until the glue is dry and then add the others so that they just touch the work surface. Some models may balance quite well on two flat shells. However, not many shells have a really flat surface so it is best to try to include a third point of contact. You could, for example, add a walking stick to a figure.

This wolf has two small feet which would not provide good balance. Three-point support has been achieved by giving him a walking stick. If you do not want to include a walking stick, the model should be mounted on a suitable base.

Scene 3

THE BIG BAD WOLF TURNS ARISTOCRAT

In this scene, the smartness of the old wolf's clothing is depicted by using light-coloured shells, although the eyes remain black. The eyes are peristomes, one of which is glued to the base of a Chinese hat shell that represents a monocle. The hat is made up of a peristome with a necklace shell on top. Notice how you can alter the facial expressions of the wolf by using the versatile oyster shell. The body is a large dog whelk, the forearms and thighs are wentletraps, and the calves (or knee-high boots) are tusks. A piece of polished oyster shell covers the back.

The model of Little Red Riding Hood is similar to that in Scene 1, but her hood and cloak are Baltic tellins. Her skirt consists of twelve pink thin tellin valves and five small orange scallops.

This big bad wolf has bulging eyes to emphasize his nasty nature.

Pose is an important element in the design of shell models. Here, Little Red Riding Hood leans forwards to give the poor old beggar a few coins.

Scene 4

THE NASTY WOLF TRIES THE CHIVALROUS APPROACH

Here, the nasty wolf is trying the chivalrous approach. He is made with very pale shells, although he still has a hint of black – very dark nassas form his ears and similarly-coloured, truncated top shells form his eyes. However, his wide open mouth, revealing his large teeth, tells the true story.

Little Red Riding Hood's short skirt is represented by a flat winkle and her hood and cloak by two misshapen pink scallop valves. Tusks form her long legs and her shoes are mangelias with rissoa heels.

Scene 5

THE WOLF PRETENDS TO BE A BEGGAR

In this scene, the wolf is an old, crippled beggar forced to travel around in a cart. The oyster shells for his mouth are very irregular. One of his eyes is a peristome; the other, which is closed, is a green sea urchin. Single netted dog whelks are used for his short legs, two more make up his tail and wentletraps make up his arms. A small Chinese hat shell is glued to the tip of one of the arms as a begging bowl.

Comforting this pitiful beggar is a lively young Little Red Riding Hood. Her body is a dog whelk on to which are glued two queen scallop valves to represent the hood and cloak. Notice how the hollow side of the shell for the cloak is turned upwards to emphasize her pose. The skirt is made with orange scallop valves. First, glue five shells, hollow side down, in a rose shape. When this part of the skirt is rigid, glue on the legs at an angle to indicate that she is leaning forward. Finally, add more shells all round on the underside to increase the size of the skirt.

Scene 6

THROUGH THE LOOKING GLASS

For this gallant wolf, two small acteons form the eyes. Four dark-coloured wentletraps form the arms. The thighs are netted dog whelks and the calves are wentletraps. The body is a cone shell. The musketeer-style hat is a saddle oyster valve with a truncated grey top glued into the hollow side. Two rounded fragments of a gastropod make a plume. The base is a solid trough shell valve whose shape emphasises the bowing pose.

Fifteen pink thin tellin valves, larger and more brightly coloured than those used in other scenes make up Little Red Riding Hood's skirt. Her hood is the tip of a crab claw, giving her the appearance of a peasant girl. Her body is a colourful cone shell and her cloak is made with a purple-red Queen scallop valve. A piece of polished, black oyster shell serves as a base.

The mirror is made entirely from yellow-tinted tusks. Work the mirror on a flat surface and assemble the shells with the wide ends glued over the narrow ones. Use small peristomes to join the mirror to the stand.

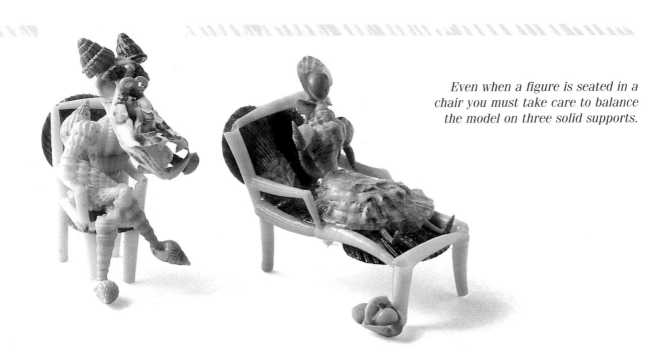

Even when a figure is seated in a chair you must take care to balance the model on three solid supports.

Scene 7

DOCTOR WOLF

The doctor's armchair is made from tusks and scallop valves. Start by assembling two tusks together to form each of the two long uprights. Lay a scallop valve (the chairback), hollow side down on the work surface and then glue the two long uprights on either side. Glue two short tusks to the top and bottom of the chairback. Glue the hinge side of a smaller scallop valve to the chairback to form the seat. Frame the seat and build the arms with more short tusks. Finally, glue on the two front legs, remembering the advice about three-point contact given on page 55.

The couch is made in much the same way as the armchair. Glue pairs of tusks together to form the two sides of the couch. Join the front end with another tusk. Glue two overlapping scallop valves to the frame to form the cushions. Fix the legs to the four corners. Assemble the back by gluing two scallop valves, side by side, to the rear part of the couch. Frame the back with three tusks and then glue the arms to the sides of the frame.

Doctor Wolf's eyes are pheasant shells with two peristomes, glued side by side, to make a pair of spectacles. Teeth are not prominent in this model, but the doctor does have a pipe made from a cerith and an acteon. The body is a netted dog whelk, the arms and thighs are wentletraps and the lower legs are tower shells. When building models such as this, it is best to assemble the head, body and thighs, fix this structure to the chair and then add the arms and legs.

Little Red Riding Hood's skirt is a convex oyster valve, only slightly polished by the sea and still retaining its flaky streaks to denote the folds in the garment. Glue the legs under the skirt before fitting it to the couch.

Witches

These figures are all made of dark-coloured shells – browns, dark greys and blacks. Choose old, slightly eroded shells with holes in them.

For each of the witches, netted dog whelks are used for the upper arms, tower shells for the forearms and crab claws for the fingers. Their faces are circular pieces of cowrie shell into which fine detail has been added.

The inside of the mouth is a piece of pearly shell. A peristome represents the tongue and the gums, and small pieces of shells the broken teeth.

The hooked nose is made of a piece of cowrie. Add a wart or two by gluing on a tiny rock barnacle or necklace shell.

The eyes are two round, truncated pieces of shell which can be glued with the hollow side inwards or outwards. Witches often have thick eyebrows and these can be depicted with pieces of sting winkle.

For the hair, use large number of small ceriths and/or tower shells. You can also use rock barnacles glued on to a saddle oyster shell.

Lots of fragments of shells have been used to make these models and it is impossible to make identical copies. You will have to work with your own collection of shells, using these models as inspiration. With a little imagination you can create a whole host of cackling hags.

Glossary

aperture   Part of the shell of a gastropod through which the animal emerges.

apex   The point at the end of the spire of a gastropod – the starting point of shell growth.

back   With gastropods, this is the part opposite the aperture. With bivalves, it is the edge where you find the umbo, ligament and hinge.

bivalve   Shellfish whose shells are composed of two hinged valves, for example a mussel or oyster.

columella   Central pillar of a gastropod's shell. The term is often used in this book to describe the central part of the shell, which is left after erosion by the sea.

ears   Growths situated either side of the hinge of certain bivalves, such as the scallop.

gastropod   Shellfish, such as winkles or whelks, whose shell is coiled in a spiral.

hinge   The part of a bivalve where the valves are joined together.

ligament   Organic matter that holds the two valves of a bivalve together when the shell is open.

peristome   The edge of the aperture on a gastropod.

umbo   The beak or point on each valve of a bivalve. Corresponds to the apex of a gastropod.

valve   Each of the two parts of the shell of a bivalve.

ventral edge   With bivalves, the part opposite the back.

Index